THE COVENANT CONNECTOR

by

Creflo A. Dollar Jr.

The Covenant Connector
ISBN 1-885072-13-9
Copyright © 1997 by Creflo A. Dollar, Jr.
Creflo Dollar Ministries
P.O. Box 490124
College Park, GA 30349

TABLE OF CONTENTS

Introduction   4

The Earth Is The Lord's   6

The Tithe Is Holy   9

Naked Before God   12

The Order of Melchizedek   15

Will A Man Rob God?   24

Gross or Net?   31

The Accursed Thing   33

Hidden Among Their Own Stuff   38

The Devourer Rebuked   49

Jesus, The Firstfruit   54

Tithing The Tithe   58

Conclusion: It's Manifestation Time   66

INTRODUCTION

Tithing brings about manifestation.

The manifestation of God's glory is the visible, tangible, physical evidence that the Word of God is operating in your life. It's when what you've read within the pages of the Bible is reflected in you and on you. When you have manifestation, no one has to wonder whether or not the promises of God have been kept, because you're the very picture of healing, prosperity, deliverance and soundness.

It's time for us as the Body of Christ, to see touch and experience all that the Bible says we can have. It's not enough for us to just come and hear the Word. We all know how important hearing is, *(Romans 10:17)* but I'm talking about that touchable "there it is" manifestation coming to pass in our lives.

The Spirit of God spoke to my heart and said, **"If folks are going to enter into abundance, manifestation or promotion, they're going to have to sow until there's a breakthrough."**

Child of God, there are three things that will hinder the manifestation of God's glory in your life — not tithing, strife and faithlessness. Of these three, tithing is an area that has not been adequately dealt with from God's perspective — until now.

Some of you are believing God for, and confessing change of status in certain situations and circumstances. When you don't tithe, you cut yourself off from the promises of God, and in effect, stand in the way of your own blessings. Although you have rights as a Christian, you can cancel your own rights by not tithing.

In this in-depth study of tithing, we'll search the scriptures from both the old and new testaments to find out just what God has to say on the subject. You will see that tithing is not something your pastor has made up for his benefit, but instead is something God requires. I'll explain what tithing is, how it's done, the benefits of tithing and the consequences of not tithing. I've even included declarations of repentance you can make to show God you've turned your back on the sin of withholding the tithe.

There have been times in the past when I've taught on this subject at our church, and a few of the members got offended and left. When I preach against adultery or reefer smoking, the only ones who get upset are the people who are smoking reefer, those who are in adultery, or both. Likewise, when I preach on tithing, the people who get upset are those who are not tithing. When you touch on areas of people's lives where they are not living according to the Word, they tend to get defensive. If tithing is one of those areas for you, allow the Word of God to mature you. Allow what He has to say on the subject, fix what needs to be fixed in your life. There is no condemnation for those of us who are in Christ Jesus, *(Romans 8:1)* but there is restoration and growth. You're never going to change until you recognize that the first step is to get in the presence of God's Word. You'll know you're mature in the things of God if you don't get offended by what you read in this book.

Make a quality decision to get all that God has promised you, *And in all your getting, get understanding. (Proverbs 4:7 NKJV)*

THE EARTH IS THE LORD'S

For the earth is the Lord's and the fulness thereof. (1 Corinthians 10:26) We are owners of nothing, but called to be faithful stewards of all that God blesses us with. *For we brought nothing into this world, and it is certain we can carry nothing out. (1 Timothy 6:7)* In other words, everything on the face of this earth belongs to God. Everything. There is absolutely nothing we brought into this world, and there is likewise nothing we can take with us when we leave. As simple as that is to grasp when it comes to most material things, Christians have traditionally been unable or unwilling to accept that idea when it comes to what they label as *their* money. The truth of the matter is, God has blessed you with whatever increase you obtain, and requires only that you return to Him the tithe, or ten percent of your increase.

To tithe is to give back to God ten percent of what He has given to you. Inherent in our willingness to tithe is the acknowledgment of God's ownership of everything in the earth, including our finances. Therefore, the tithe should be an expression of your appreciation and thanksgiving to God for what He has done in your life. It should not be seen as a burden or a loss, but should be seen as the opportunity it is for you to prosper in the things of God.

And all the tithe of the land, whether of the seed of the land, or of the fruit of the tree, is the LORD'S: it is holy unto the LORD.

And if a man will at all redeem aught of his tithes, he shall add thereto the fifth part thereof.

And concerning the tithe of the herd, or of the flock, even of whatsoever passeth under the rod, the tenth shall be holy unto the LORD.

He shall not search whether it be good or bad, neither shall he change it: and if he change it at all, then both it and the change thereof shall be holy; it shall not be redeemed.

These are the commandments, which the LORD commanded Moses for the children of Israel in mount Sinai. (Leviticus 27-30-34)

Notice in the first verse we are told that the tithe belongs to the Lord. It is not yours or mine to do with whatever we choose, because it doesn't belong to us, it belongs to God. In *Proverbs 3:9* we are instructed to *"Honour the LORD with thy substance, and with the firstfruits of all thine increase."* The substance of our finances is what we are to honor the Lord with, thanking Him for the provision to have our needs met. The firstfruits are equal to the tithe. So anywhere in the Bible where it refers to firstfruits, you know that also belongs to the Lord.

Now, if you're a good businessman, you know the tithe of your business belongs to God. Only ninety percent of your business is yours, and the firstfruits of all your profit should be presented as tithes in honor to the Lord. As a Christian, only ninety percent of your time is yours. The remainder should be spent in time of prayer, fasting and communion with God. Likewise, your body is the temple of the Holy Spirit, on loan to you from above. It was purchased with a price, and on the day of Judgment, you will have to give an account of how you carried yourself.

What I need for you to see Child of God, is that tithing is not an option. It is not something that has been put up for a vote, for us to decide whether or not it is the right thing to do. No, God says that the firstfruit, the initial ten percent of your increase is His. It is dedicated and set aside for His use. Folks come up with all sorts of reasons as to why they should not, could not or would not tithe. They say things such as, "Well, it's an Old Testament thing, and since it's not mentioned in the New Testament, we don't have to tithe." Others try to justify not tithing by saying that "God surely is not moved by something as basic as money." The problem is that up until now, we've not understood God's heart on this subject, and in so doing, have missed out on the blessings we're supposed to inherit through tithing. Working our way through scripture, we will prove that tithing is a biblical mandate, a covenant issue and an opportunity to honor God. Victory in your life is determined by how you handle the tithe.

THE TITHE IS HOLY

As we discovered in the previous chapter, the tithe is holy. It belongs to the Lord, and it is holy. Being holy has nothing to do with how you dress. It's not in outward things. Holiness is the state of being in agreement with God. It is the state of being of one mind with God. To be holy is to find out what the Bible says, and to be in agreement with what God says.

In the Old Testament, there was something else deemed holy and sacred unto God, and that was the Ark of the Covenant. This sacred, portable chest — along with its two related items, the mercy seat and cherubim — was the most important, sacred object to the Israelites during the wilderness period. Also known as the Ark of the Lord, it was the only article of furniture in the innermost room, or Holiest of Holies of Moses' tabernacle and of Solomon's temple. This was something so special, that a person could not just touch it irreverently. It was so holy, that even if you touched it unintentionally you would die. In the Bible, the word "death" is literally translated as a separation. And, when a man touches the tithe, or mishandles the tithe, separation from God takes place.

When you're holy, whatever the Bible says is wrong is what you say is wrong. Whatever the Bible says is right is what you say is right. If the Bible says that behaving in a certain way is sin, well, that's what you say is sin. That's holiness.

Now, when He says the tithe is holy, and we understand the definition of holiness, then we begin to see the tithe as the thing that keeps us in agreement with what God has promised. God has given us a covenant, and then He has given us this system called tithing, which is an avenue by which we maintain or break the agreement. To tithe is to maintain the agreement between you and God. On the contrary, to not tithe is to break agreement with God. Tithing the tithe is the process by which you present your tenth to Jesus, our High Priest — the Author and Finisher of our faith. When you are tithing the tithe, you are constantly confirming your agreement with God, and with the covenant promises attached to the tithe.

The problem most people have with Leviticus 27, is that it's in the Old Testament. Because it is located in that portion of the Bible, most people will say they don't have to receive that as a commandment from God, and believe that we are governed only by the New Testament.

Well folks, this is what I perceive concerning this New Testament, Old Testament issue. If we are not obligated to keep the entire Bible, then God would have only given us the New Testament. You may have been led to believe that since some publishers only print those little green Bibles that only include the books from Matthew to Revelation. Now, we do live under the New Testament, but the Old Testament is a foreshadowing and a foundation. It acts as a column to hold up the beliefs and confirm the position of the New Testament.

But how obligated are you? Is this just an Old Testament issue? Can you just ignore the commandments about tithing because you consider yourself a New Testament Christian? Well now, let's back up a little bit. Let's go to the book of Genesis and answer this question. Let's decide once and for all if this is an Old Testament issue or if it is a covenant issue.

The second chapter of Genesis begins the saga of a man by the name of Adam. He was, as you may know, the first man we see in the restructuring of the earth. I didn't say he was the first man on the earth, but that's a discussion for another book, another time. God is talking to Adam. He gives him the garden, authority, and all these other neat things and makes promises of what is to come. Then in ***Genesis 2:16-17*** He says:

"...Of every tree of the garden thou mayest freely eat:

But of the tree of the knowledge of good and evil, thou shalt not eat of it: for in the day that thou eatest thereof thou shalt surely die."

Well, in fact, he could only eat ninety percent of the garden. God specifically told Adam not to eat of the dedicated tree. God was telling Adam that they would be able to maintain the agreement they had, just as long as Adam did not touch that which was God's. The success of their agreement was based upon whether or not Adam touched the dedicated thing. As far as God was concerned, if that happened, the agreement was off, and He would have to separate from Adam.

You're probably saying, "He did eat of the tree, and the Bible says he was going to die, but yet he lived several hundred more years." There was still a death, a separation that took place in that situation. The glory that Adam had been walking in, the promise to walk like God and be like God was over. He touched God's stuff. And, since he touched God's stuff the agreement was off — not to be reinstated until someone came along to redeem the crime.

NAKED BEFORE GOD

Now, Adam was in agreement with what God had said, but then we go to *Genesis 3:6:*

And when the woman saw that the tree was good for food, and that it was pleasant to the eyes, and a tree to be desired to make one wise, she took of the fruit thereof, and did eat, and gave also unto her husband with her; and he did eat.

When the woman ate of the tree, I don't believe anything irreversible happened. I believe that the agreement was still in effect because God had made the agreement with Adam, and not with his wife. But here, we see the woman leading by influence when she should have been following. She should have been helping, aiding and supporting, but not taking the lead. A woman by nature has the tendency to want to lead things. When things aren't getting done properly, she just wants you to get out of the way so she can take care of things. And by nature, most men will sit back and let her do what she wants. That's why as men, we have to guard against that fleshly desire of the woman to want to lead, and the casual attitude of men to want to just sit back and let her take over. The problem is that when you let a woman stay in that place for too long, she'll get used to it. Then you come to church and find out it's the man who is supposed to be leading. Now, it's going to take an act of Congress for you to reclaim your God-given authority.

I believe even if the woman had taken the fruit and eaten of it, and Adam reminded her that they were in agreement with God, things would have turned out differently. He should have said, "We can only eat of the ninety percent. I will not touch that which is God's. You need to go somewhere privately and pray, Sweetheart. In the meantime, I'll go to God and intercede on your behalf before we lose our coats of glory, and have to run around naked." Instead, he was seduced by her influence.

After they ate, they knew they were naked. Prior to that they were without artificial clothing, but they were beautifully clothed in the presence and the glory of God. A separation then took place, and they had to sew fig leaves together to hide their shame. All of a sudden the glory that had covered them, the glory that had sustained them was off because somebody touched God's stuff.

I wonder how many of you reading this book are naked today before God? I wonder how many of you are naked of the glory, naked of the provision, and naked of manifestation because you've touched God's tithe? You went out and spent God's money on a new dress. You're clothed in artificial clothing, but you're without the power, promise and anointing of God — all because you touched the tithe.

At one point, I got carnal with God on this and I said, "Come on now, God. Just between me and you. I mean, the man didn't do anything but bite off of a piece of fruit. I mean, how are you going to throw the earth into the chaos of sin, just because he bit some fruit? I didn't even read that he had two bites. One bite apiece of the fruit caused You to get upset like this?" What I heard in my spirit was this: **"That's not the point. The point is that we had an agreement. That tree was the only thing that stood between Me doing what I said I would do, and Me not being able to do what I said I would do. I want to fulfill My promises, but I cannot lie. When you break the agreement, it's broken. I can't come up like some human beings do and say, oh, that's all right. Because if I did that, all Heaven and earth would pass away. My Word is true. In this case, that tree was the only thing standing**

between the agreement being intact, and the agreement being broken."

After this, God had a dilemma. They touched the tithe and the glory was off man. He needed a method by which to mend the situation, and get the promises back to mankind. So now, He's looking for a man with whom He can cut covenant. If you know anything about the story of Cain and Abel, you would know that Abel would have qualified. He was a covenant-keeping man and also a tither, but Cain killed him. At this point, God is still looking for someone with whom to cut covenant. He's still looking for someone who would tithe.

Which brings us to the twelfth chapter of Genesis, and to a man by the name of Abram. He sends Abram to a place where there is famine, and He makes good His promises to him. There is a transference of wealth into Abram's hands in subsequent chapters.

THE ORDER OF MELCHIZEDEK

Now the LORD had said unto Abram, Get thee out of thy country, and from thy kindred, and from thy father's house, unto a land that I will shew thee:

And I will make of thee a great nation, and I will bless thee, and make thy name great; and thou shalt be a blessing:

And I will bless them that bless thee, and curse him that curseth thee: and in thee shall all families of the earth be blessed. (Genesis 12:1-3)

The word "bless" means to empower you to prosper, or empower you to excel. Then, He demonstrated what He had just promised. That's what covenant is all about. A covenant is a pledge, a vow, a promise between two or more parties to carry out the terms agreed upon. A covenant can only be broken by death, when it is made in blood. We don't need to make agreements of that sort today because we have the blood of Jesus, but back then this was the strongest type of agreement known to man. All throughout the following chapters, we see God making and confirming His promises to Abram, whose name was changed to Abraham.

And I will make thy seed as the dust of the earth: so that if a man can number the dust of the earth, then shall thy seed also be numbered. (Genesis 13:16)

Follow me to the fourteenth chapter when Abram's brother was abducted:

And there came one that had escaped, and told Abram the Hebrew...

And when Abram heard that his brother was taken captive, he armed his trained servants, born in his own house, three hundred and eighteen, and pursued them unto Dan.

And he brought back all the goods, and also brought again his brother Lot, and his goods, and the women also, and the people. (Genesis 14:13-14, 16)

Abram had been in battle, won the battle and received the spoils of the battle. Pay close attention to what Abram does with his increase.

And Melchizedek king of Salem brought forth bread and wine: and he was the priest of the most high God.

And he blessed him, and said, Blessed be Abram of the most high God, possessor of heaven and earth:

And blessed be the most high God, which hath delivered thine enemies into thy hand. <u>And he gave him tithes of all</u>. (Genesis 14: 18-20)

Look what's happening Child of God, right in the middle of this covenant being made, we see this man bringing in the tithe. Now, let me put this in your spirit: <u>Wherever you find a tither, you're going to find victory. Wherever you find a non-tither, you're going to find failure. The covenant promises of God can always be produced for someone who will continue to stay hooked up to the covenant through his tithes</u>.

And the king of Sodom said unto Abram, Give me the persons, and take the goods to thyself.

And Abram said to the king of Sodom, I have lift up mine hand unto the LORD, the most high God, the possessor of heaven and earth.

That I will not take from a thread even to a shoelatchet, and that I will not take any thing that is thine, lest thou shouldest say, I have made Abram rich... (Genesis 14:21-23)

What's he saying? "I don't want anything from you. I'm going to continue to tithe. I'm going to give my firstfruits to God, and no one will be able to say they made me rich, but

God Himself." In the following chapter they're getting ready for the covenant ceremony. Abram wanted to know how he would inherit all the things God promised him. Prior to that in Genesis 15, the Bible tells about the various animals needed for the ceremony, and the process of cutting the actual covenant. *In the same day the LORD made a covenant with Abram, saying, Unto thy seed have I given this land..." (Genesis 15:18)* Then they go into chapter 17, and He says something fascinating about this covenant which answers the question so many of you have about whether or not this is an Old Testament issue.

And I will make thee exceeding fruitful, and I will make nations of thee, and kings shall come out of thee.

And I will establish my covenant between me and thee and thy seed after thee in their generations for an everlasting covenant, to be a God unto thee, and to thy seed after thee. (Genesis 17:6-7)

God changed Abram's name to Abraham when the covenant was cut between them. If tithing is a part of that covenant making process between God and Abraham, and the Bible says this is an everlasting covenant, then who else is included in the covenant? According to the scripture you just read, you are. In *Galatians 3:29* the Bible says, *"And if ye be Christ's, then are ye Abraham's seed, and heirs according to the promise."* That means everything God promised Abraham, He also promises to you. Through the High Priest, He promised Abraham that He would bless him to be a blessing. Abraham brought the tithe to the High Priest and he was blessed. Bringing the tithe was the avenue by which Abraham could partake of the covenant promises of God.

Here is what most of us in the Body of Christ have a tendency to do. We sings songs about Abraham's blessings being ours, but we seem to forget how he got the blessings. You see, you can't get the promise unless you get it through the method demonstrated in Genesis 14:18 when it says, "blessed by Abram of the most high God" — a confirmation of what He promised to do earlier. It is through this tithe that God was able to carry out His promise of blessings to Abraham. Since Abraham represents all of us, if we do what he did, then we can get what God promises in our lives the same way Abraham got them to operate in his life. All of these promises put together comprise the Abrahamic Covenant. Since the Bible says that this covenant is everlasting, there is no end to the vows made or to the blessings promised. With that in mind, does it end in 1997? Will it end in the year 2,000? Will it end after we've been raptured? No, because everlasting means without end. So, if tithing is part of the Abrahamic Covenant, does it make a difference that you read about it in the Old Testament? No, it doesn't. It's part of an everlasting covenant which transcends and which breaks the boundaries of the New Testament. For those of you who think that we modern day Christians have only to live by the New Testament, I say this: We are covenant people. Not only do we live by the New Testament, but we are also heirs of the Abrahamic Covenant, and anything in the Old Testament that is part of the promise God made to Abraham, is applicable to our lives today! So, whoever tells you that tithing is not for today, and that it was just for the old covenant saints is mistaken. You need to quickly take them through the Word of God and show them that tithing is part of an everlasting, forever covenant that pertains to us even today. And, God requires us, if we want Abraham's promises in our lives today, to tithe the same way Abraham did in his day. Follow me so far? With all the scriptures I've given you, I know in my spirit that some of you are still fighting the idea of giving back to God ten percent of what belongs to Him. That spirit that tries to talk you into hanging on tightly when the Bible clearly tells you to let go and let God, is a demonic spirit based on the love of money. The Bible says in the book of

Timothy, that the love of money is the root of all evil. But, do you know what that really says when it talks about the love of money? It's about having the wrong relationship with the material world. Inside of you right now, if you have a funny feeling that this Georgia preacher is trying to talk you out of giving ten percent of your money to your local church, you're under the influence of a demonic spirit. I can't make it any plainer than what you've read. You can't even accuse me of giving you my own interpretation, because I just led you through the Bible.

"Well Brother Dollar, I might be inclined to believe you if you could show me this in the New Testament."

I'm glad you brought that up. Turn to **Luke 11:42**. Notice that it's Jesus talking here. You can tell because it's written in red.

"But woe unto you, Pharisees! for ye tithe mint and rue and all manner of herbs, and pass over judgment and the love of God: <u>*these ought ye to have done,*</u> *and not to leave the other undone."*

They're tithing all of these different things. He said "You tithe, and you ought to." Jesus Himself is telling them that they ought to tithe, but added that when they tithe they are not to omit the weightier matters, such as the love of God and judgment. You can't act like a fool and tithe. There are other things you must consider. You have to be faithful to the Word of God if you're going to be a tither. Jesus says you ought to tithe.

If you're wondering why I haven't yet taken you to Malachi, just be patient. We'll get to Malachi in a minute. You may not want to even go to Malachi after what you're about to read. You may not ever want to read Malachi again as long as you live. You may even be inclined to tear that book out of your Bible after you read what's coming up.

So also Christ glorified not himself to be made an

high priest; but he that said unto him, Thou art my Son, to day have I begotten thee.

As he saith also in another place, Thou art a priest for ever after the order of Melchisedec. (Hebrews 5:5-6)

Wasn't this Melchisedec the same high priest Abraham brought his tithes to? Here the scripture is saying that Jesus is a High Priest forever — after the order of Melchisedec. Just what is He saying here? That Jesus is a High Priest, and that He will operate in the same manner Melchisedec operated in. So, that means if we want to know about Jesus' priesthood and how it is to operate, all we have to do is find out how Melchisedec's priesthood operated. What we know is that <u>Melchisedec received the tithe!</u>

Who in the days of his flesh, when he had offered up prayers and supplications with strong crying and tears unto him that was able to save him from death, and was heard in that he feared;

Though he were a Son, yet learned he obedience by the things which he suffered;

And being made perfect, he became the author of eternal salvation unto all them that obey him;

Called of God an high priest after the order of Melchisedec. (Hebrews 5:7-10)

The Bible further defines this order by which Jesus' priesthood is to operate. *Whither the forerunner is for us entered, even Jesus, made an high priest for ever after the order of Melchisedec.*

For this Melchisedec, king of Salem, priest of the most high God, who met Abraham returning from the slaughter of the kings, and blessed him;

To whom also Abraham gave a tenth part of all; first being by interpretation King of righteousness, and after that also King of Salem, which is, King of peace;

Without father, without mother, without descent,

having neither beginning of days, nor end of life; but made like unto the Son of God; abideth a priest continually.

Now consider how great this man was, unto whom even the patriarch Abraham gave the tenth of the spoils.

And verily they that are of the sons of Levi, who receive the office of the priesthood, have a commandment to take tithes of the people according to the law... (Hebrews 6:20, 7:1-5)

Here is the order. You've got to have the tithe, the person who presents the tithe, and a high priest to receive the tithe. And, some way or another, He's got to be able to return a blessing back to the tither. All along we've thought that you just give the tithe and that's it. Any time a tithe is given the tither is empowered. Tithing the tithe is the process by which you present your tenth. This is done by speaking over the tithe before you sow it, planting it into the kingdom. We present the tithe with words, our High Priest takes the tithe, looks over the promises and returns the promise for the tithe. He'll bless you in the same way He blessed Abraham. If you've got a sick body and you're standing on the promise of healing, then you ought to take that tithe that day, in what the Bible calls your evil day, and present it to the High Priest, Jesus. Go to Him and say, **"I present to You my tithe, in the name of Jesus. I speak to You and say that You are a Healer in my life."** He takes the tithe, looks back over the agreement and says, "There's healing here. I've got the tithe. You've got the promise. Put healing back on her because she gave the tenth." Please hear and understand me, God's promises being kept are all based on how you handle the tithe. Jesus is the High Priest over the covenant.

And verily they that are of the sons of Levi, who receive the office of the priesthood, have a commandment to take the tithes of the people... (Hebrews 7:5) They are commanded by law to take tithes. That indicates to me that

God is using the priest to receive His tithe. That's interesting. According to this, the only people who could go in the presence of the covenant were the high priests. I can just imagine what would happen, if someone was to decide he was just as anointed as the priest, and go into the Holiest of Holies. What would happen is that his dead body would have to be dragged out. Before he went in, even the priest would tie a rope around himself with a bell attached. As long as folks could hear the bell, they knew everything was all right. But if he went in there and the bell stopped ringing, everyone would know that the priest must have messed up that week. They would pull him out by the rope and find a new priest. Sin cannot survive in the presence of the Almighty God. In those days you didn't see everyone and his cousin claiming to be called into the ministry.

...that is, of their brethren, though they come out of the loins of Abraham: (Hebrews 7:5b)

When God made that promise, even though they were yet in the loins of Abraham, that promise affected them as well.

But he whose descent is not counted from them received tithes of Abraham, and blessed him that had the promises.

And without all contradiction the less is blessed of the better. (Hebrews 7:6-7)

That's why Jesus has to be our High Priest. No one is ever going to be better than Him. But now the less, you and I, when we give our tithes will be empowered to prosper and to excel by the better. It's His job to carry out the promise. The order of Melchisedec is the process of tithing. Skeptics and people who prefer not to tithe will insist that the subject of tithing doesn't appear in the New Testament. However, if you're not aware of what the order of Melchisedec is, you won't know that the Word on tithing does indeed appear when Jesus is on the scene. For years people who cannot rightly divide the Word have been telling you that it doesn't appear past Malachi.

Speaking of Malachi, let's go there. Here's where it gets a little personal. At this point, do you believe that tithing is the will of God? After reading this book, how many of you say you're going to practice this for the rest of your life? Only God knows for sure. Some of you are probably saying you'll never read another one of my books again because I took up all these pages to talk about the tithe. You're probably complaining that you don't have enough money now to even pay your bills, and here I am talking about returning ten percent of what you receive. <u>Believe it or not, tithing is not a money issue, it's a covenant issue</u>. If you want the things of God, such as finances to pay your bills, you have to obey His Word.

This is how you go about changing from being a non-tither to a tither. First of all, you get yourself in an atmosphere where the Word is going forth. Don't go to a church and get in an atmosphere where you're just shouting and having a good time. That won't get your bills paid. The only way for you to change is to get the Word with understanding. If you don't understand the Word that's going forth, you haven't gotten it in your spirit. Whenever I preach a sermon, your getting is based on whether or not you understood it. There are plenty of preachers preaching sermons that people aren't getting. They may be exciting, but no one knows what was said. After reading this book, you should be able to go out and explain tithing to someone else. If you can do that, I've done my job. If you can't, read the book again.

WILL A MAN ROB GOD?

Malachi 3:3
And he shall sit as a refiner and purifier of silver:
and he shall purify the sons of Levi, and purge them as
gold and silver, that they may offer unto the LORD an
offering in righteousness.

Righteousness is a covenant word. Whenever you hear someone talk of their right-standing with God, or their rights in God, know that they are speaking about covenant. So what this scripture is saying is that they may give an offering according to the covenant. Realize this Child of God, to give an offering is to make an offer. Just because you make an offer, doesn't mean that the offer has been accepted. I can offer you $100 for your car and it's actually worth $5,000. Just because I make an offer to you doesn't mean that you have to accept it. Likewise with God. What do you think about on Sunday mornings when you bucket plunk your $2.50? What would you say if I told you that maybe, just maybe, He didn't accept it? What we need to know as Christians is when an offering is accepted and when it is rejected, because as I said earlier, not all offerings are received. That may be a reason why you have yet to see manifestation in your life. Here you are walking around thinking that you have seed in the ground, and perhaps God didn't take you up on your offer. You're thinking that you're giving God a memorial offering, and He's saying "No, you can't offer Me this because it's not offered according to covenant. It's not being offered in righteousness."

Then shall the offering of Judah and Jerusalem be
pleasant unto the LORD, as in the days of old, as in former
years.

And I will come near to you to judgment; and I

will be a swift witness against the sorcerers... (Malachi 3:4-5)

Sorcery. Just what do you think all that's about? The 1-900 psychic line stuff, that's what that's all about. He says I'm going to be a witness against those sorcerer types.

...and against the adulterers, and against false swearers, and against those that oppress the hireling in his wages, the widow, and the fatherless, and that turn aside the stranger from his right, and fear not me, saith the LORD of hosts. (Malachi 3:5)

For I am the LORD, I change not; therefore ye sons of Jacob are not consumed.

Even from the days of your fathers ye are gone away from mine ordinances, and have not kept them. <u>Return unto me, and I will return unto you</u>, saith the LORD of hosts. But ye said, Wherein shall we return? (Malachi 3:5b-7)

He's referring back to Abraham when He speaks of the days of your fathers. That word "ordinance" means order. He says, you have gone away from My order. Now, you can't help but ask here, "What order is He talking about?" When He says return, you can't return something that wasn't there in the first place. When He says "return" that is a clear demonstration of exchange, and that's what covenant is all about. There's always an exchange in covenant. There's an exchange of weaknesses for strengths. He said, "Now you return to Me, and I'll return to you." In other words, there are some things that should be exchanged here. Some things that are no longer being exchanged because of something that has not been returned.

<u>Will a man rob God?</u>... (Malachi 3:8)

Answer that question. Will a man rob God? The answer is an emphatic, yes! Have you ever robbed God? He's referring to what He's getting ready to explain as a robbery. There is such a thing as God-robbing. And, what you have to ask yourself is this: Am I, Christian that I am, a God-robber? Glory to God! You don't want to get to the gates of Heaven, only to have your records show you're guilty of robbing God, do you?

Yet ye have robbed me. But ye say, Wherein have we robbed thee? *In tithes and offerings*. (Malachi 3:8b)

You've robbed Him of the tithes, because that's His money — not yours. But He didn't stop at the tithe. That's what got to me. He said "Not only are you guilty of robbing Me of the tithe, you're also guilty of robbing Me of the offering."

Two robberies. One is bad enough, but He has accused us of being guilty of a double transgression.

Understand that the way you rob Him of the tithe is to not give it up. By keeping it in your wallet and putting it among your stuff. That's simple enough to figure out. But, the offering? "Come on God. Don't you remember? I know it wasn't much, but I gave you $2.50 last week. Surely, You remember that?"

You may have been giving an offering, but the offer you made was not given according to covenant. **An offering is not received by God until it is given over and above the ten percent!** Simply stated, you cannot give a legal offering until you first of all give a legal tithe. You can't do it, because it's illegal. God will reject your offering if you have not first committed unto Him the tithe, which is rightfully His. And, while you're trying to put seed in the ground to get manifestation, God says, "I don't receive it because it's not presented according to righteousness, and it's not pleasant to Me."

Let me put this another way. My congregation blessed me with a Rolls Royce during a recent pastor's appreciation. Say for example, I give you my Rolls to drive, you keep it continually and give me $10 each week for gas. I don't want $10 from you. I want my Rolls back. Give me my Rolls back. But each week, you come to me with the $10, and I reject the money. It's the same way with God. Each week you come and give Him a few dollars, and it's a stench in His nostrils. He doesn't want the offering until you have proven to be faithful over the tithe. His attitude is, since you're not giving the tithe, He's not giving you deliverance, prosperity or peace. He's not giving you anything His Word says you can have because you're still holding on to something that belongs to Him. Everything stops until you give God back what is rightfully His. Then, He's able to return some things to you.

Don't get upset and put the book down. God has provided a way out for you!

It could be that your blessings are locked up in Heaven because His stuff is locked up in your bank account. I know this may come as a hard saying to you, but no offering is received by God if you're not a tither. That's just the plain, simple truth. Despite what you've been told in your church. Now watch this:

Ye are cursed with a curse: for ye have robbed me, even this whole nation. (Malachi 3:9)

If you were to get hold of a Hebrew Bible, you would see that this last scripture says, "I give you final notice of the cancellation of our contract." It's just like when an insurance company sends you a notice of cancellation for not paying your premiums. If you're in an accident, they're not required to come and bless you because you kept what was theirs, according to the contract you signed.

So, God is putting you on notice. Every time you hold on to the tithe, He's sending you a notice in the mail that your contract is about to be terminated.

Bring ye all the tithes into the storehouse, that there may be meat in mine house, and prove me now herewith, saith the LORD of hosts, if I will not open you the windows of heaven, and pour you out a blessing, that there shall not be room enough to receive it. (Malachi 3:10)

I've heard that the storehouse is a man of God, but I take issue with that statement. I believe Jesus is the storehouse. A storehouse is a place where all the resources and supply come from. The supply first of all comes from God to the church, and is then distributed. As a man of God, I can't give anything unless if is first given to me by God. I'm the distribution center. The storehouse is the One Who has the supply and can operate as a supplier. I can only distribute that which comes into my hands. Distributor status comes after you've proven yourself in the stewardship department. Most people think that a person is automatically a steward because they sow seeds into the kingdom. The Bible says, ***"Moreover it is required in stewards, that a man be found faithful." (1 Corinthians 4:2)***

God will not choose you to be a steward, will not make you a distribution center until you're found faithful over that with which He has entrusted you. You must pass the test of faithfulness. He will not give you that which is your own until you have shown yourself faithful over that which is another man's. *(Luke 16:12)*

God sends the supply and your pastor in turn can give the supply to you. As long as the Word of God is going forth from the pulpit of your local church, that's where your needs are being met. The Word of God is the needful thing. Just because you turn on the television and someone thrilled you and caused chill bumps to appear on your arms, that's not an indication to send money designated for your local church, across the country to some televangelist. He is not the one who feeds the Word to you constantly. Suppose the program is canceled, then what? Unless God tells you to tithe to a television ministry, your sowing should be done in home soil. Just because you like what you see on television, that is not an indication that's where your tithes are to be sent. Now, if you're not getting fed in your local church, you need to pray and ask God for direction as to where you should be attending.

For those of you who attend megachurches and have a problem with not being able to shake the pastor's hand, remember this: Your pastor did not die on the cross for you, Jesus did. Therefore, you don't come to church to meet some man, you come to hear the Word of God. I've even heard some people say that because they pay their tithes, they have a right to meet personally with the pastor. If you read your Bible, you would know that Moses was rebuked by his father-in-law for attempting to govern so many people by himself. A word from God came to him to appoint counselors over the people and divide them up into groups. We use this system in our own church and it works well. The only counseling I do is from the pulpit. When my members come to church faithfully, they get the answers they need from my sermons. If that doesn't work, I have a catalog of tapes on just about the widest range of biblical subjects available. Get in your mind that you don't pay tithes to meet with the pastor. It's not an admission ticket, it's tribute and thanksgiving to God. You don't pay tithes to the pastor. The tithes don't belong to any man, the tithe belongs to God. You don't pay tithes to get a personal audience with your pastor, you pay them to be blessed of God. Don't make the mistake of making your pastor your source, because if he's human, chances are God is not through with him yet. Make God your source. If you spend quality time in the Word, and time going to church, and time praying in the Holy Spirit in a faithful manner, you won't need to have anyone counsel you but Jesus, Himself.

God is making you an offer you cannot refuse. Bring the tithe and watch Me open the windows of Heaven. Bring the tithe and watch what I can do for you. When our church first started with eight members, every one of them were tithers. The power of God was all over the place. When the church began to grow, manifestation decreased. I asked the Lord why, and He told me this: **"What happened was that before,**

you had one hundred percent tithers and the windows were opened one hundred percent. Then the crooks started coming in. Those who wanted the Word, but didn't want to pay. God-robbers started joining the church. They hooked up with you and affected the whole nation, and the windows closed down to eighty percent." At that point, we only had eighty percent tithers, which means eighty percent manifestation. It has gone steadily downward as the number of people joining the church has increased. The manifestation we need is being held up on account of the thieves, the ones who would dare to rob God.

GROSS OR NET?

People always ask if they are to tithe off the gross, or off the net income of their paycheck. Tithes are taken from the increase, and what you are increased by is the gross. The net only appears because the government doesn't trust you enough to send them their ten percent, so they take it out before you get it. If you purchased a car for $3,000 and then turned around and sold it for $3,000 do you tithe off of that? No. Why? Because there was no increase in that situation. On the other hand, if you purchased a car for $3,000 then sold it for $3,500 you are responsible for tithing off the additional $500 increase. You would tithe $50 from that transaction. If there's an increase, there's a tithe. If you should happen to borrow money, there's no requirement to tithe because there is no increase. You've just incurred a debt that must be repaid. Now, you've put yourself in the position of being a servant to the one who loaned you the money. *(Proverbs 22:7)* Also, when you receive an income tax refund, it is not necessary to tithe on that since the government is refunding the over and above they took from you throughout the year. This is money that you should have been tithing on all along, so there's no need to tithe on it again.

The tithe is the covenant connector. It connects you to the covenant promises of God. No matter what you tithe, covenant law says that's what you will get in return. If you sow time, you'll get time. If you sow service, you'll get service, and if you sow money, you'll get money. **God can provide a harvest from your tithe in the form of favor, a raise, a monetary gift, bonus or any other type of financial increase.** The tithe is what will hook you up to the many promises of God. Just as God told Abraham in the Old Testament to establish His covenant, He is telling you to do the same thing, Child of God. When you establish His covenant, God will cause manifestation to occur in your life. Bring the tithe and the promises will come. Whenever you touch the tithe, you touch the covenant. Whenever you honor the tithe, you honor the covenant. In all the years I've been born-again, I've never understood the seriousness of tithing until now. I never associated the tithe as that which connected me to the promises of God until now. I realize like never before that if healing is promised to you in His Word, not tithing will hinder that covenant of healing from ever coming on your body. If you find in the Word where God has promised you protection, then tithing will guarantee that you get that protection you were promised.

Don't let your wrong relationship with the material world stop you from getting what's yours. You hear a sermon on tithing, and the first thing that happens is that you become fearful that the preacher is trying to get your money. The fear comes in and the devil puts you in a position where the promises of God can't come to pass in your life. Satan doesn't care one way or another about the money, but he does care about you getting what God has promised you. So you operate in fear that the Word of God will not come into your life where the benefits of tithing are concerned, and so you don't tithe. You then make this fear a self-fulfilling prophecy because since you're not tithing, the Word of God cannot operate to bring you the blessings God has promised.

THE ACCURSED THING

Just how serious does God take this issue of tithing? I've heard people say that God with all of His love, and all of His mercy and kindness is not going to allow you to suffer because you neglected to bring in the ten percent to the storehouse.

In this chapter, I will show you exactly what God understands about those who transgress His Word where the tithe is concerned. Go with me to the book of Joshua, the sixth chapter, and we'll begin this aspect of the discussion with the walls of Jericho. As a child in Sunday school, all I knew was that someone walked around that wall seven times. It wasn't until recent revelation did I come to understand that tithing is a part of this story.

In this context of scripture, they refer to the tithe as the "dedicated" or "accursed" thing. The word "accursed" means devoted or dedicated, so when you read scripture that talks about the accursed thing, it is referring to the tithe. In those days they called the tithe the accursed thing because to touch something that belonged to God would bring a curse on you. It was accursed because it represented what would happen to you if you made the mistake of touching God's stuff. Notice everything that is going on in these verses in Joshua, and to where the verses are leading.

Joshua 6:1-16

Now Jericho was straitly shut up because of the children of Israel: none went out, and none came in.

And the LORD said unto Joshua, See, I have given unto thine hand Jericho, and the king thereof, and the mighty men of valour.

And ye shall compass the city, all ye men of war,

and go round about the city once. Thus shalt thou do six days.

And seven priests shall bear before the ark seven trumpets of rams' horns: and the seventh day ye shall compass the city seven times, and the priests shall blow with the trumpets.

And it shall come to pass, that when they make a long blast with the ram's horn, and when ye hear the sound of the trumpet, all the people shall shout with a great shout; and the wall of the city shall fall down flat, and the people shall ascend up every man straight before him.

And Joshua the son of Nun called the priests, and said unto them, Take up the ark of the covenant, and let seven priests bear seven rams' horns before the ark of the LORD.

And he said unto the people, Pass on, and compass the city, and him that is armed pass on before the ark of the LORD.

And it came to pass, when Joshua had spoken unto the people, that the seven priests bearing the seven trumpets of rams' horns passed on before the LORD, and blew with the trumpets: and the ark of the covenant of the LORD followed them.

And the armed men went before the priests that blew with the trumpets, and the rearward came after the ark, the priests going on, and blowing with the trumpets.

And Joshua had commanded the people saying, Ye shall not shout, nor make any noise with your voice, neither shall any word proceed out of your mouth, until the day I bid you shout; then shall ye shout.

So the ark of the LORD compassed the city, going about it once: and they came into the camp, and lodged in the camp.

And Joshua rose early in the morning, and the priests took up the ark of the LORD.

And seven priests bearing seven trumpets of rams' horns before the ark of the LORD went on continually, and blew with the trumpets: and the armed men went before them; but the rearward came after the ark of the LORD, the priests going on, and blowing with the trumpets.

And the second day they compassed the city once, and returned into the camp: so did they six days.

And it came to pass on the seventh day, that they rose early about the dawning of the day, and compassed the city after the same manner seven times: only on that day they compassed the city seven times.

And it came to pass at the seventh time, when the priests blew with the trumpets, Joshua said unto the people, Shout; for the LORD hath given you the city.

So far, everyone should know what this series of scriptures is about. God gave Joshua and his folks command to walk around the city once a day for six days, and on the seventh day to walk around the city seven times. The wall was to supernaturally fall, tumble down, and Joshua and his men were to go in and possess the city. But now, watch this:

And the city shall be accursed, even it, and all that are therein, to the LORD: only Rahab the harlot shall live, she and all that are with her in the house, because she hid the messengers that we sent.

And ye in any wise <u>keep yourselves from the accursed thing, lest ye make yourselves accursed,</u> when ye take of the accursed thing, and make the camp of Israel a curse, and trouble it.

But all the silver, and gold, and vessels of brass and iron, are consecrated unto the LORD: they shall come into the treasury of the LORD. (Joshua 6:17-19)

As you can see, Rahab the harlot was allowed to live because she hid the spies Joshua had sent in to check things out. Because of the covenant, she is being blessed as she blessed the man of God. And, while the men are being told what to do in order to see victory, they are given a warning about the accursed thing and told to stay away from it. The accursed thing is the tithe of the silver, gold, brass and iron, and they belong to God. Just as in these verses of scripture, the tithe is brought into the treasury of the Lord. The only thing that can bring about defeat for us as well as Joshua's people, is the mishandling of God's belongings. On the other hand, we are guaranteed to live a victorious life if we honor the Lord with the firstfruits of all our increase and substance.

So the people shouted when the priests blew with the trumpets: and it came to pass, when the people heard the sound of the trumpet, and the people shouted with a great shout, that the wall fell down flat, so that the people went up into the city, every man straight before him, and they took the city. (Joshua 6:20)

That is the victory they were after, so obviously they handled the tithe correctly. Obviously, no one touched the devoted thing. In the upcoming verse, we see the harlot Rahab and her father's household being blessed.

And Joshua saved Rahab the harlot alive, and her father's household, and all that she had; and she dwelleth in Israel even unto this day; because she hid the messengers, which Joshua sent to spy out Jericho. (Joshua 6:25)

This particular promise came to pass for Rahab because Israel honored God with the dedicated thing, and as I have tried to show through scripture, this is what connects you with the promises of God. The promise being, *I will bless those that bless you, and curse those that curse you.* **(Genesis 12:3)** This clearly demonstrates how victory can come into your life when you honor God with the tithe. On the other hand however, let's see if you really want to continue to spend God's money by mishandling the tithe. You'll find that it just may be better for you to forego that trip to the mall, and give God what is rightfully His.

HIDDEN AMONG THEIR OWN STUFF

Go with me now to *Joshua 7:1:*
But the children of Israel committed a trespass in the accursed thing...
Uh-oh, somebody sinned.   Somebody touched the tithe.
...for Achan the son of Carmi, the son of Zabdi, the son of Zerah, of the tribe of Judah, took of the accursed thing...
Achan has gone and taken of the tithe.   Is your middle name Achan? Some of you may have to answer that question by faith. Go ahead and say no, we'll just call those things that be not as though they were. *(Romans 4:17)*
...and the anger of the LORD was kindled against the children of Israel. (Joshua 7:1b) You can put your name in here if you're taking the tithe. You wonder if it makes God angry if you don't tithe? Of course it makes Him angry when only a small percentage of the church is bringing the tithes to the storehouse. He can't accomplish what He wants to accomplish in the local church, because of the crooks touching the accursed thing. Then what happens is that you have people wondering if God is on the job because they can't see the power of God operating in peoples' lives. Yes, it makes Him angry. Read on:
And Joshua sent men from Jericho to Ai which is beside Bethaven, on the east side of Bethel, and spake unto them, saying, Go up and view the country. And the men went up and viewed Ai.
And they returned to Joshua, and said unto him, Let not all the people go up; but let about two or three thousand men go up and smite Ai; and make not all the

people to labour thither; for they are but a few. (Joshua 7:2-3)

So, the spies came back and said, "We shouldn't have a problem taking these folks. There are not that many of them. There's no reason why we should trouble ourselves. Just send a few thousand."

So there went up thither of the people about three thousand men: and they fled before the men of Ai.

And the men of Ai smote of them about thirty and six men: for they chased them from before the gate even unto Shebarim, and smote them in the going down: wherefore the hearts of the people melted, and became as water. (Joshua 7:5)

What happened here is that big, bad Israel came into battle thinking they would easily wipe out this people who should not have been a problem, only to have 36 men quickly destroyed and chased back from the gate.

And Joshua rent his clothes, and fell to the earth upon his face before the ark of the LORD until the eventide, he and the elders of Israel, and put dust upon their heads.

And Joshua said, Alas, O Lord GOD, wherefore has thou at all brought this people over Jordan, to deliver us into the hand of the Amorites, to destroy us? would to God we had been content, and dwelt on the other side Jordan! (Joshua 7:6-7)

In other words, "God, why did you bring us over here to get our butts kicked?"

O Lord, what shall I say, when Israel turneth their backs before their enemies? (Joshua 7:8)

What a cowardly act. His men looked like sissies as they ran away from the enemy. What was he going to say to all the people who were sure to bring up this incident?

And the LORD said unto Joshua, Get thee up... (Joshua 7:10)

That sounds like some of us. Crying to God and asking why He let our lights get turned off. "And, what about an air conditioner? It's so hot outside, and my house is burning up with heat. Oh, God I don't even have a car. I'm so tired of walking. My body is sick, and I just got laid off. Where are you anyway God? How come I'm not healed?"

Israel hath sinned...(Joshua 7:11)

Does it shock you that God would call touching the tithe a sin? Most of you don't even consider it a sin because you consider it your money. You think that you have the right to do with the tithe whatsoever you will, but the Bible says, that God looks at a man who spends the tithe as a sinner.

...and they have also transgressed my covenant which I commanded them: for they have even taken of the accursed thing, and have also stolen, and dissembled also, and they have put it even among their own stuff. (Joshua 7:11)

All righty then. This is the picture. They have sinned against the covenant. And, in so doing, God is not able to bring His promises to pass in their lives. He promised victory, healing, deliverance and prosperity but He can't give them those things. They obviously didn't see the direct relationship between the covenant and the dedicated thing.

How about you? Have you taken God's tithe and put it amongst your own stuff? You've deposited 10 percent in your bank account when it should have gone into God's treasury. And if it is amongst your stuff, just how many times have you done this very thing? How many times have you mingled your things with God's things? The tendency most of us have is to justify stealing the tithe by saying, "I worked and earned this money." But the Bible has made it very clear. All of the tithe of the earth is the Lord's. What you don't seem to understand is that if it were not for God, there would be no earth, no air, no you — so He's entitled to all of the tithes of the earth. Think about it. Without God you wouldn't be here, you would be nothing were it not for Him. He's just trying to take care of His business, and you have the audacity to try to justify not giving God what is rightfully His. Tell me Job, did you form yourself? Just how would you breathe without the oxygen God supplies? The utility company will turn off your lights if you don't pay them. Yet, God is still allowing the sun to shine on the just and the unjust. Don't tell me He is not a merciful God. If He wasn't, He would cut your oxygen off every time you didn't tithe. Don't tell me He's not kind and loving. It's just that He has to honor the covenant. God has to do His part, but we have to do our part as well. God is not going to break His covenant. It comes with blessings <u>and</u> curses.

Therefore the children of Israel could not stand before their enemies, but turned their backs before their enemies, because they were accursed: <u>neither will I be with you anymore, except ye destroy the accursed from among you</u>. (Joshua 7:12)

For all of you who are non-tithers, I wonder how difficult a time you're having standing against your enemies. You can't stand up against sickness or disease. You can't stand up against the pressures of this world so you cave in, give up, quit and backslide. Under normal circumstances you would be able to handle these things, but something that was once sweatless now becomes an ordeal. All because you have God's stuff mixed in with your stuff. That dress you're wearing, if it's brought with the tithe, you know of course that it's stolen merchandise. I hope that weave you're sporting wasn't purchased with God's tithe, because if so, it's <u>really</u> not your hair, but God's.

One thing most people never realize is that when you rob God, redemption has to take place. The Bible gives you the option of going to God in repentance to ask for forgiveness. It says in *1 John 1:9, "If we confess our sins, he is faithful and just to forgive us our sins, and to cleanse us from all unrighteousness."* At least you have the option of going to God and talking to Him about it. The children of Israel didn't have that same option. God told them point blank, "I'll not have anything to do with you until you destroy the accursed from among you." That was their only option. He told them if they did not find the person who touched the devoted thing and destroy him, He was not going to have anything else to do with them. Now Child of God, that's serious.

I wonder what would happen if God were to do that today? Can't you see how much mercy we're operating under? Suppose God were to say, "All right, don't tithe, see if I care, I quit. I'm not going to have anything to do with you until you fix it." Many of you are living lives where you've not repented of those times you robbed God because, every time you thought to do the right thing, you felt as if you weren't able to tithe because you couldn't see how you were going to make it until the end of the month. The irony of that is that if you'd start doing what He requires of you, He'd be able to show you some things you couldn't see. The very reason you can't see until the end of the month is because you're robbing from God, and His wisdom is cut off from you. The children of Israel have only one way out of this situation:

Up, sanctify the people, and say, Sanctify yourselves against to morrow: for thus saith the LORD God of Israel, There is an accursed thing in the midst of thee, O Israel: thou canst not stand before thine enemies, until ye take away the accursed thing from among you. (Joshua 7:13)

You have enemies folks! The devil is your adversary. He wants you dead, poor, messed up and confused. The Bible says if you're not tithing, you can't stand against your enemies. Satan is not your friend. He will never be your friend. He wants you pitiful and in Hell. He wants to be able to laugh at you when everything is over and done with because you're in Hell with him.

So Joshua rose up early in the morning, and brought Israel by their tribes; and the tribe of Judah was taken: (Joshua 7:16)

And he brought his household man by man; and Achan, the son of Carmi, the son of Zabdi, the son of Zerah, of the tribe of Judah was taken.

And Joshua said unto Achan, My son, give, I pray thee, glory to the LORD God of Israel, and make confession unto him; and tell me now what thou hast done; hide it not from me.

And Achan answered Joshua, and said, Indeed, I have sinned against the LORD God of Israel, and thus and thus have I done: (Joshua 7:18-20)

Even Achan knew he had sinned, but we have Christians who touch the tithe and act as if they have not done anything wrong. As if is their right to spend all that comes into their hands.

When I saw among the spoils a goodly Babylonish garment, and two hundred shekels of silver, and a wedge of gold of fifty shekels of weight, then I coveted them, and took them; and, behold, they are hid in the earth in the midst of my tent, and the silver under it. (Joshua 7:21)

This is what some of us will do. You see the money you can keep for yourself. You see that you're giving money to the church that you could've used to pay your light bill, or bought a new dress or suit, and you coveted it. When you covet something, you want to possess and own something that is not yours. This is what God was speaking to Moses about when He warned him not to covet anything that was his neighbor's. When you covet something you don't release it. You try to take hold of something that doesn't rightfully belong to you. In this instance, Achan has the stuff hidden at his house. If I were to ask you today where God's stuff was, you'd probably say it's in the bank, or under your mattress, or hidden in your shoe.

I don't know about you, but I am moved by what I read in these scriptures. What you need to understand is that at one point in my life, I didn't believe in tithing. I felt as if I had worked too hard to get the little money I had, only to have some preacher stand before me and tell me I had to give up ten percent. That was one of those "no compute" situations for me, until I woke up. And, I'm not just talking about waking up in the spiritual sense, either. I mean I literally woke up one morning and went outside to find that someone had thrown a brick through the window of my brand new car. The first thing I asked was, "God, why did this happen?" And He said, **"The devourer came in, just like he was supposed to."** All of a sudden, I got the revelation of the scripture that promises He will rebuke the devourer for my sake. *(Malachi 3:11)* Guess when I became a tither? I didn't want the devourer taking anything from me. When that happens, the money you're trying to hold on to is going to leave anyway, because you've got to replace something that was lost, stolen or broken. One way or another you're going to lose it. What goes around comes around, and if you're stealing what belongs to God, someone or something is going to steal what belongs to you. Lord have mercy!

So Joshua sent messengers and they ran unto the tent; and behold, it was hid in his tent, and the silver under it.

And they took them out of the midst of the tent, and brought them unto Joshua, and unto all the children of Israel, and laid them out before the LORD. (Joshua 7:22-23)

At this point I was thinking, praise the Lord, it's all over, but it wasn't over at all. Remember, God had already told them that He would not be back until they destroyed the person who had touched the tithe. That's what God said. Let's just imagine what it would be like today if God had not given us the grace and mercy we're presently under. We'd probably have a computer system that you would have to access before you came into the church. In order to get in, you would insert a card that would lift the entry gate. If you were not a tither, you would be arrested in the lobby, and brought down to stand before the church. The ushers would then hand out rocks and guns to everyone. Probably Uzi's. We'd say "Jesus" three times and then we would shoot all the non-tithers. Once all the transgressors were dead, God would come back into our place of worship, and we could have church. On the program each Sunday would be time set aside for picking out all of the crooks and getting rid of them so God could come into the place. We don't realize how fortunate we are to be under this modern system.

This man's sin even affected his entire family. They were all being judged because the head of the household transgressed the covenant. Let me tell you something men. Don't depend on your wife to bring the tithe, you personally make sure the tithe gets in. That's your job as a man of God, and head of your household. Your family can either be blessed or cursed based on how that household is handling the tithe. I'm telling you that God is very serious about this. Although my wife and I are tithers, we got a revelation of just how serious this thing is during a storm in our neighborhood. We had set the tithe aside, but had not yet sown it. You see, you can have the tithe, and have funds designated to tithe, but seed that has not been sown has not been deposited into the kingdom. I woke up the next morning to find that the shingles from my roof were littering the neighborhood. I took a drive through our subdivision to see what kind of damage the other houses had sustained. No one's house had been damaged, but mine. I said, "Lord, the man of God's house?" Shingles everywhere. "What's up with that?" Then I remembered as the Lord spoke to me clearly saying, **"You haven't made your deposit. No deposit, no return!"** Think back to the scripture in Malachi where He says, *"Return unto me, and I'll return unto you."* Here we were waiting on our return, and God was waiting on His too. So, while we were waiting, the devourer came in and did some devouring. As soon as we both realized what we had neglected, we got that tithe in right away. A confirmation of the importance of sowing the seed came months later when another storm hit the neighborhood, and everyone's house was damaged but ours.

Now, getting back to Achan. This may be a bit hard for some of you to accept, but Achan's sons, daughters and even the family pets were about to suffer for something Achan neglected.

And Joshua, and all Israel with him, took Achan the son of Zerah, and the silver, and the garment, and the wedge of gold, and his sons, and his daughters, and his oxen, and his asses, and his sheep, and his tent, and all that he had: and they brought them unto the valley of Achor.

And Joshua said, Why hast thou troubled us? the LORD shall trouble thee this day. And all Israel stoned him with stones, and burned them with fire, after they had stoned them with stones.

And they raised over him a great heap of stones unto this day. So the LORD turned from the fierceness of his anger. Wherefore the name of that place was called, The valley of Achor, unto this day. (Joshua 7:24-26)

This probably seems barbaric and cruel to some of you, but this is exactly what was required in those days when someone made off with what belonged to God. Notice, the Lord turned from his anger only after they got rid of the one who had touched the accursed thing. In chapter eight, the Lord returns the victory and covenant promises to Joshua and his gang.

And the LORD said unto Joshua, Fear not, neither be thou dismayed: take all the people of war with thee, and arise, go up to Ai: see, I have given into thy hand the king of Ai, and his people, and his city, and his land: (Joshua 8:1)

And the LORD said unto Joshua, Stretch out the spear that is in thy hand toward Ai; for I will give it into thine hand. And Joshua stretched out the spear that he had in his hand toward the city. (Joshua 8:18)

And Joshua burnt Ai, and made it an heap for ever, even a desolation unto this day. (Joshua 8:28)

As soon as the tithe situation was straightened out, everything else fell into place. Failure and defeat, victory and success are all based on how a person sows that ten percent of his increase. It should be clear to you by now that you can be connected or disconnected from the promises of God based on how you handle the money. And, you wonder if this is a serious issue. The New Testament says, in **Luke 16:11, "If therefore ye have not been faithful in the unrighteous mammon, who will commit to your trust the true riches?**

No servant can serve two masters: for either he will hate the one, and love the other; or else he will hold to the one, and despise the other. <u>Ye cannot serve God and mammon.</u>" *(Luke 6:13)*

This clearly is not just an Old Testament issue, but as we discussed earlier, it is an issue of the covenant between you and God.

When people start to argue you with over the biblical requirement to tithe, don't go there with them. Just give them a copy of this book. Pay them to read it if you have to. Anything so that their minds can be renewed to a subject about which the devil has not wanted the Body of Christ to get a revelation. Don't turn the subject of tithing into a debate where strife and contention can be brought in, because that will cancel your manifestation. If people choose to ignore biblical teaching after it's been brought to their attention, there's nothing you can do about that. They obviously want to stay poor, broke, busted and disgusted. There's no need for that, because the Bible has a better way. No matter how much money you plant, if you're not a tither you're not going to find that hook-up. And remember, you first have to get to the ten percent before you can offer the eleven percent, which is where the offering starts.

THE DEVOURER REBUKED

Let's go back to the book of Malachi for a moment, where God is making reference to what He'll do as far as the devourer is concerned.

Bring ye all the tithes into the storehouse, that there may be meat in mine house, and prove me now herewith, saith the LORD of hosts, if I will not open you the windows of heaven, and pour you out a blessing, that there shall not be room enough to receive it.

And I will rebuke the devourer for your sakes...(Malachi 3:10-11a)

That word "rebuke" means stop, no more! If you're being devoured, bring the tithe and present it before God. He says, He'll make the devil stop taking from you. You have a right to go to God and say, **"Lord, I bring this tithe right now in the midst of all the Hell that I'm in, and I stand on Your Word. I give you this tithe. You said in Your Word that You will rebuke the devourer for my sake. Now, I expect this situation that's on me to stop right now. I know it's my fault. I know I brought this all on myself, but Lord, make it stop right now in the name of Jesus."**

If you're getting tired of losing every job you get, bring the tithe. If your car has been repossessed, or you've been evicted from your home, bring the tithe. Bring it and God will make the devil stop harassing you.

... and he shall not destroy the fruits of your ground; neither shall your vine cast her fruit before the time in the field, saith the LORD of hosts. (Malachi 3:11b)

Perhaps you've been working and laboring to get certain

things to happen in your life, and it's just not happening. When you don't tithe, the devourer has every right to destroy the fruits of your ground. You may even have fruit come up, but it doesn't last long. You can make plenty of money, but still not be able to tell where it's going. When my wife Taffi and I were starting a family, I made sure that my tithes were given consistently. I was not about to have the enemy cause any of my children to miscarry, in the name of Jesus. In fact, we had to *make* all of our children come out, because they were very comfortable where they were. God will not allow the fruit of your body to be cast out before its time. If you're one of those women who gets pregnant only to lose your baby, there are several things you need to examine in your life. First of all, are you and your husband tithing? Secondly, check to see if there is strife in your household, and thirdly, check out any biological issues that may be causing you to miscarry. In fact, you can take your tithe and sow that tithe and say, **"In the name of Jesus, I have a right to the fruit of my body. Now, I rebuke whatever is going on here, and in the name of Jesus I line my life up with the Word of God. I thank you God that my baby is full term and healthy."**

Sow for a baby if you and your spouse want one. Don't give up. Be specific. Put your order in and thank God in advance for your child. Forget about getting depressed over this issue. Depression is not of God. Every time you partake of your marital duties, invite the Holy Spirit into that setting, and thank God in advance for conception taking place. There were people in the Bible who didn't have children until the anointing of God showed up. How about the Shunammite woman Elisha came across? She had been waiting for a baby for a long time, and Gehazi told Elisha that she was barren.

And he said, About this season, according to the time of life, thou shalt embrace a son. And she said, Nay, my lord, thou man of God, do not lie unto thine handmaid.

And the woman conceived, and bare a son at that season that Elisha had said unto her, according to the time of life. (2 Kings 4:16-17)

Well, just like Elisha, I'm not lying when I tell you that the anointing will do what you've been trying to get done all these years. The anointing will remove that burden of childlessness if you don't give up, cave in and quit on God. Every time you tithe you need to put God in remembrance by saying, **"Lord, this is my tithe. This is my covenant connector, and I bring it before You right now, and I thank You for conception and for my child. Be it unto me, according to Your Word."** If you're walking in doubt, think about Mary. She was told she was going to be pregnant and she had never even known a man in the biblical sense. With the anointing of God, all things are possible.

And all nations shall call you blessed: for ye shall be a delightsome land, saith the LORD of hosts.

Your words have been stout against me, saith the LORD, Yet ye say, What have we spoken so much against thee? (Malachi 3:12-13)

Tithing is done with words, so make sure you don't use words to stop your seed. Speak in line with the promises of God. Don't disconnect yourself from the covenant by speaking words that will stop those blessings in their tracks. Words can stop what the tithe has released.

Ye have said, It is vain to serve God: and what profit is it that we have kept his ordinance, and that we have walked mournfully before the LORD of hosts? (Malachi 3:14)

Here's an example of what you say that will stop your tithe from producing a harvest for you: "Here I am tithing, and I see this drug dealer driving a better car than mine." Your words will stop what the tithe is trying to bring to you.

"Oh well, I don't understand. I'm bringing my tithe to

the church, riding in an old, beat up Toyota, and the preacher is riding in a Rolls Royce." There go your words again. If your preacher is riding in a Rolls, you need to thank God that he is, because that means you too can have one. Don't let your mouth stop you from reaping the blessings your tithe will hook you up to. Just continue to think of that ten percent as your covenant connector. Glory to God.

"Yeah, I hear you Brother Dollar, but what am I to do if I've been robbing God?"

We can take care of that right now. I've got a declaration you can make to get rid of that crook spirit that is causing you to rob your Father in Heaven. If you make a commitment to never rob Him of the tithe again, I believe He'll forgive you of the debt.

"Heavenly Father, I am convinced by Your Word that tithing is a Word issue. It is a covenant issue, and it is the will of God. Therefore, in the name of Jesus, I will not transgress the covenant I have with You. Neither will I rob you of the tithe any more for the remainder of my life. I ask you Lord, to forgive me. I confess that when I touched the tithe, I sinned. But Your Word says, that If I confess my sins, You are faithful. You are just to forgive me of all my sins and to cleanse me from all unrighteousness. Thank You Lord for forgiveness. Thank You Lord for the promises. I walk in them now, and I boldly declare that the covenant connector is a permanent part of my life. In Jesus' name. Amen."

If you will, just take time out to worship God over the teaching and newly found understanding you have of this subject. Go to Him in prayer and tell Him that you come before Him honoring Him with the tithe of everything that is increased in your life. Ask the Lord to connect you with every promise His Word gives to those of us who love Him. Ask to be connected to the promise of healing, the promise of deliverance, the promise of abundance and the promise of prosperity. Ask that everything He's ever promised in His Word be connected to you this day. Give God the glory, the praise and the honor. Thank Him for commanding the devil to stop devouring that which is rightfully yours. Thank Him for opening doors that no man can shut, and for bringing forth favor in your life. Those things you've been dreaming of and wondering why they haven't come yet, thank God that they are coming now in the name of Jesus.

Don't hold on to your tithe, sow it as quickly as it comes into your hands. Whatever you do, don't get into fear and bondage thinking that the pastor, the finance director or someone counting the money will take your tithe and use it for purposes other than what God intended it to be used for. Your confidence is that you've done what God commands of you. Woe be it unto the person who then steals what you have brought to Jesus, your High Priest, in reverence and obedience. As you read earlier in this book, God has His own special way of dealing with robbers. Once you've sown your tithe, don't even allow the fear of the devil to rob you of the joy of your righteousness.

JESUS, THE FIRSTFRUIT

Before you can qualify for a promise to be fulfilled in your life, someone has to give a tithe. No tithe, no promise. God had promises that He wanted to give to us where resurrection was concerned, but resurrection cannot be given to everyone unless a tithe is given. **Romans 11:16-18** says:

For if the firstfruit be holy, the lump is also holy: and if the root be holy, so are the branches.

And if some of the branches be broken off, and thou, being a wild olive tree, wert grafted in among them, and with them partakest of the root and fatness of the olive tree...

Boast not against the branches. But if thou boast, thou bearest not the root, but the root thee.

The Amplified Version of the Bible says it like this:

Now if the first handful of dough offered as the first fruits [Abraham and the patriarchs] is consecrated [holy], so is the whole mass [the nation of Israel]; and if the root [Abraham] is consecrated [holy], so are the branches.

But if some of the branches were broken off, while you, a wild olive shoot, were grafted in among them to share the richness [of the root and sap] of the olive tree,

Do not boast over the branches and pride yourself at their expense. If you do boast and feel superior, remember it is not you that support the root, but the root [that supports] you.

Child of God, what root is supporting you? Is it a root that has broken agreement with the covenant of God, or is it a root that's responsible for hooking you up with the covenant? I'm convinced that the reason most people are not seeing manifestation of what God has promised is directly related to the tithe. You don't have a right to His promises. The agreement has been called off because of your decision to hold on to the money. Why are you going to God to ask Him for anything when there's no agreement?

But now is Christ risen from the dead, and become the firstfruits of them that slept.

For since by man came death, by man came also the resurrection of the dead. (1 Corinthians 15:20-21)

Christ became a tithe. God wants ten percent of your firstfruits. Chances are if you do tithe, you pay your bills first and if you have some left over you'll do what God commands. What you're supposed to do is get your paycheck, tithe, and if there's anything left over, you are to pay your bills. If there's none left over, then you have the confidence that *my God will supply all of your need according to his riches in glory by Christ Jesus. (Philippians 4:19)* He can't do that if you don't connect first. It amazes me to hear people say they can't afford to tithe. In that case, you also can't afford to get healed, to prosper or to be delivered. That's what you're saying. You're saying that you can't afford to have any of the blessings promised to Abraham.

That means you can't afford to have peace in the midst of your storm. You can't afford longsuffering, or the anointing. Every promise in the covenant is predicated on your connection with the covenant through your tithes. Even if you're on welfare, you can afford to tithe —unless you want to stay on welfare for the rest of your life. God needs a bridge, He needs a way to funnel blessings to you. As an example, God presented Jesus as a tithe for all. God saw fit to tithe one man in the ground, get one man to die and have us all connected to the promise of being raised from the dead. Adam's mishandling of the tree in the Garden of Eden caused death, a separation from God for everyone. Jesus came to connect mankind back to God.

There are non-tithing people who get up in the morning to experience a sweet hour of prayer and my question to you is, why? God is not in your hour, and it certainly isn't sweet if He is not there. Non-tithing people come to church, lifting up holy hands during praise service because they want to get in the presence of God. Don't you understand that He's not there? In our church, we don't have praise team members who are not tithers. We have a report that tells us such things. We don't want any praise team person trying to lead us into God's presence, when they've already been kicked out. They're not connected to God. I don't want some God-robber trying to lead the congregation into worship. What happens in that instance, is since they don't have the presence of God, they rely on their talent. Talent never has and never will remove burdens and destroy yokes, only the anointing can do that.

Here's something for you to think about. There is a difference between what a tither hears in church and what a non-tither hears. While a tither is hearing me talk, at the same time, the Holy Spirit is speaking to them. When I open my mouth to say something, a person who is a tither has already picked up on what I'm about to say, because we're connected. They've connected to the promise of revelation knowledge exploding on the inside of them. All the while the non-tither sits there looking at his watch, as if he doesn't understand what's so exciting about the message. He sees me as a preacher reading scriptures that are boring him out of his mind. That person can only sit there and hope that I will soon be finished with the sermon. But, right behind him is the person who is excited and obvious in his excitement over the Word. Those who choose not to connect, are those who don't have a clue as to what is going on. He's trying to fight sleep, and anxious to leave because nothing is happening on the inside of his spirit. The tither however, is tuned in and hearing his way out of sickness, poverty, disease and trouble. He has a right to a way out.

If you're wondering about mercy, yes, it's still here but I'd rather live in the blessings of God, than for someone to have to intercede for me and beg God to show me mercy. There are certain things I have a right to by way of my agreement with God. That's what righteousness is. People think they can neglect the things of God then fall back on grace and mercy. Grace is not just unmerited favor. The full definition of grace is God's willingness to get involved with you. Grace is not to be misused because you've misinterpreted it, but it is an anointing that produces favor. When God shows up to do you a favor it's because you got in the place where favors are found. This is the set time for favor, and God can increase you in things you've not even asked for because you're connected to the promises. He just wants to do something for you because you showed up!

TITHING THE TITHE

Tithing the tithe is done with words. God has given us specific instructions on how to give the tithe. It's not just supposed to be thrown in a bucket — that's called bucket-plunking. God expects that we will pray His Word over the firstfruits with which He has blessed us, before putting it in the hands of our High Priest.

That thou shalt take of the first of all the fruit of the earth, which thou shalt bring of thy land that the Lord thy God giveth thee, and shalt put it in a basket (or put it in an envelope in this day and time), *and shalt go unto the place which the LORD thy God shall choose to place his name there.*

And thou shalt go unto the priest that shall be in those days, and say unto him, I profess this day unto the LORD thy God, that I am come unto the country which the LORD sware unto our fathers for to give us.

And the priest shall take the basket out of thine hand, and set it down before the altar of the LORD thy God.

And thou shalt speak and say before the LORD thy God, A Syrian ready to perish was my father, and he went down into Egypt, and sojourned there with a few, and became there a nation, great, mighty, and populous:

And the Egyptians evil entreated us, and afflicted us, and laid upon us hard bondage:

And when we cried unto the LORD God of our fathers, the LORD heard our voice, and looked on our affliction, and our labour, and our oppression:

And the LORD brought us forth out of Egypt with a mighty hand, and with an outstretched arm, and with great terribleness, and with signs, and with wonders:

And he hath brought us into this place, and hath given us this land, even a land that floweth with milk and honey.

And now, behold, I have brought the firstfruits of the land, which thou, O LORD has given me. And thou shalt set it before the LORD thy God, and worship before the LORD thy God.

And thou shalt rejoice in every good thing which the LORD thy God hath given unto thee, and unto thine house, thou, and the Levite, and the stranger that is among you. (Deuteronomy 26:2-11)

What these scriptures are showing us is that it is necessary to go to God in prayer, reminding Him of the promises of healing, salvation, peace, joy and all else contained in the covenant you have with Him. Picture Jesus, the High Priest, presenting your tithe before the throne of God. You now have God's attention and proof that the agreement is still in effect. This is the time to get whatever you need from Heaven. This is the time to open your mouth and speak those things you're believing God for. When you finish presenting your tithe, the Bible calls it making an end of tithing all of the tithes of thine increase.

Don't ever forget that it is Jesus you bring your tithe to, and not the preacher — not some man. The preacher may be the one collecting the tithes, but you have placed your dedicated thing before the throne of God. If someone chooses to do something stupid with your tithe after you've presented it, that's between that man and God. You've kept God's commandment, and done everything that God requires of you. Once you get it there you profess:

"Lord, I bring this tithe before You, before the covenant of promises You have made with my father Abraham, and with me, the seed of Abraham. In the

name of Jesus, I come before You putting you in remembrance of the promise to heal me of all manner of sickness and disease."

Jesus takes the tithe and puts it before God. The Bible tells you to keep on talking:

"I say unto You Lord, that I was a sinner on my way to Hell. I didn't have God on my side, and I didn't have Heaven in my view. I was in a land of bondage being defeated on all sides, But, I remember Lord, when the doctors had given up on me, how You came and changed the report. I remember how You healed me and delivered me with signs and wonders with a mighty outstretched hand. I come to You right now Lord, thanking You Lord for the promise of complete healing according to the covenant. Now, I'm connected to Your promise with my tithe. Now I worship You Lord, and I rejoice before you Lord, and I thank You Lord for all the good that You're doing in my life. Thank You for my job. Thank You that I've got a place to stay. Thank You that I'm able to inhale and exhale. Thank You that I've got a bed to sleep in, and that my family is well. Thank You Lord.

Now God, I declare in the name of Jesus, that this promise You've made in covenant is based on the tithe I've brought to You. I've connected with the promise and You've got to bring it forth. Jesus is my High Priest, after the order of Melchisedec. I believe the system set in place that says when I bring the tithe, You bring the promise. Amen."

Child of God, as you can see, the words you speak over your seed are very important. When you just throw your envelope in the bucket as it passes by, you're not taking full advantage of the power inherent in the Word of God. The wonderful thing here is that God has to respond to His Word, and by covenant law He has to go one step further than you go when you make the presentation. Take for example the circumstances surrounding Abraham's tithing the firstfruit of his flesh, his son Isaac. Jesus would not have been given as the firstfruit of resurrection if Isaac had not been offered up initially. When God set Abraham up to offer his son as a sacrifice, He was obligated by covenant to go a step further than what He had asked Abraham to do.

And it came to pass after these things, that God did tempt Abraham, and said unto him, Abraham: and he said, Behold, here I am.

And he said, Take now thy son, thine only son Isaac, whom thou lovest, and get thee into the land of Moriah; and offer him there for a burnt offering upon one of the mountains which I will tell thee of.

And Abraham rose up early in the morning, and saddled his ass, and took two of his young men with him, and Isaac his son, and clave the wood for the burnt offering, and rose up, and went unto the place of which God had told him.

Then on the third day Abraham lifted up his eyes, and saw the place afar off.

And Abraham said unto his young men, Abide ye here with the ass; and I and the lad will go yonder and worship, and come again to you. (Genesis 22:1-5)

Abraham did not talk contrary to what he had said in his tithing process. He went about talking according to his covenant. "Yeah, I know God told me to bring my son up here to kill him, but I have a promise with God and I'm connected. I know God will have to work this thing out, because He promised that my seed would outnumber the stars. Isaac will have to live so he can produce some seed himself, so God will have to do something. Either He's going to raise him from the dead, or He's got to provide something else for me to offer. I don't know how this will end, but I'm in covenant and God's got to come through because He promised. I'm not disconnecting until I get manifestation of what I've been promised, so I'll continue to talk in line with what I'm expecting. I know that me and the boy are coming back down this mountain!"

You should take lessons from Abraham. Instead, you sow your seed and walk out of the church doors saying you can't afford to go to lunch today, instead of declaring the abundance and prosperity already promised to you in God's Word. Or else you confess that you can't imagine living in that pretty mansion you just drove past. Not to worry. If you can't imagine it, you can't have it. Whatever you can imagine is what you can possess.

And Abraham took the wood of the burnt offering, and laid it upon Isaac his son; and he took the fire in his hand, and a knife; and they went both of them together.

And Isaac spake unto Abraham his father, and said, My father: and he said, Here am I, my son. And he said, Behold the fire and the wood: but where is the lamb for a burnt offering?

And Abraham said, My son, God will provide himself a lamb for a burnt offering: so they went both of them together. (Genesis 22-6-8)

Why didn't he just turn to his son and say, you're the offering? Because he wasn't moved by what he saw. He wasn't moved by his circumstances. He was not speaking based on what was actually going on, he was speaking based on the promises of God. Just in case you believe that Abraham was lying, consider this: The Bible says in *James 3:14, "...lie not against the truth."* The truth is the Word of God. There may be facts in your life, but those facts may not line up with the truth of the Word of God. So, when you have to choose what to believe, choose the Word of God and lie not against the truth of God's Word. If the doctor says you're going to die of cancer, the Bible says that by the stripes Jesus suffered at His crucifixion, you are healed. *(1 Peter 2:24)* To choose healing over what the doctor said will change the outcome of what the doctor said.

Abraham and his son came to the place where they could hook up with all that God said they could have. There is place where you can find out if you're real about those things you're believing God for. It's the place where you can quit on God and backslide, or it's the place you say that for God I live and for God I will die. I don't know if you've gotten there yet, but everyone will have to pass that test at some point in their life. Once you pass that test, you'll hear God say, **"Now, I know."** I'm thoroughly convinced that it's easy to be a Christian, when it's easy to be a Christian.

And they came to the place which God had told him of; and Abraham built an altar there, and laid the wood in order, and bound Isaac his son, and laid him on the altar upon the wood.

And Abraham stretched forth his hand, and took the knife to slay his son.

And the angel of the Lord called unto him out of heaven, and said, Abraham, Abraham: and he said, Here am I.

And he said, Lay not thine hand upon the lad, neither do thou any thing unto him: for now I know that thou fearest God, seeing thou hast not withheld thy son, thine only son from me. (Genesis 22:9-12)

Seeing that you did not withhold the tithe, seeing that you did not withhold your seed, I know now. Many of you have not gotten to the place of "now, I know" because it's easy for you to give a $2.50 tithe, but when you're increased to the point of having to tithe $2,000 — well that's another story.

And Abraham lifted up his eyes, and looked, and

behold behind him a ram caught in a thicket by his horns: and Abraham went and took the ram, and offered him up for a burnt offering in the stead of his son. (Genesis 22:13)

Instead of a lamb, God found His own tithe in the ram. The ram was the substitute, but the promise showed up just the same. God wanted Abraham to sow his fruit first, so that God could sow His. Abraham was willing to sow Isaac, even though he ended up not having to. The important thing is that he was willing. That's all God needed to know. His plan was to plant His own Son Jesus as a perpetual tithe. He knew that they were going to crucify His Son, leave Him for dead, and He would be buried. God knew that He was going to the very pit of Hell, only to rise up on the third day. Jesus was risen up the firstfruit from the dead, but if you read your Bible carefully, Jesus was not the only one recorded to have been resurrected that day. Paradise was closed the day Jesus was resurrected, and all of the captive saints came out of that place because Jesus Himself was the tithe. God Almighty is telling us to bring our tithes, so He can do something better. If you think you're giving up something, He has blessings that are exceedingly, abundantly above anything your could ever ask or think. *(Ephesians 3:20)* He says that He will heal you better, deliver you better and prosper you better — all of this through the tithe. He wants to do for you better than the world's system could ever do for you. He's just waiting for you to consistently bring your tithe with a willing heart. Our prayer should be to ask the Lord to forgive us for taking this ten percent so lightly, and treating it as nothing important. Now we know, and now we do.

This tithing thing is more serious than we've thought in the past. This is the generation during which God is making revelation so readily available. This is information that must be imparted to churches everywhere. Jesus is on His way back, and we have to have as many people victorious over the devil as possible. I believe that as we read and are taught on this subject, God is setting us up for awesome manifestation. The manifested wealth God wants to bring to us is for the purpose of spreading the gospel all over the world. God will give us the wealth to fulfill His covenant until all families of the earth have been blessed. *(Deuteronomy 8:18)*

IT'S MANIFESTATION TIME

Child of God, it's manifestation time.

If you're ever going to change people, the only way to do it is through the impartation of words. All of us are made up of words and opinions and ideas that have been imparted into our hearts by someone else. Only what is imparted from the Word of God has the power to change and rearrange our way of thinking.

I promised God that another day would not go by when I would refrain from saying something because I feared what people might think. I will never do that again as long as I stand here on earth. There are some things that need to be said. There are sensitive issues that need to be dealt with within the Body of Christ. You cannot change people by trying to deal with them through their emotions. The only way to change folks is by dealing with them through their heart, and words are the only avenue by which to get into a man's heart and bring about manifestation. I may be in jeopardy of losing thousands of members in my decision to say whatever He tells me to say, but that's all right. If I end up with just a few faithful followers of the Word of God, that's all right by me. I'm willing to take that chance, because I've got to see Jesus. God is my life. He is the source of my supply, and the source of my strength, and without Him I am nothing.

It's time for manifestation. It's time for people to see what they've been confessing, and hold what they've been reading. It's time for you to smell what you've been praying about. Listen! It's not enough for the preacher to preach a cute little sermon from the pulpit. It's not enough for you to jerk and jiggle and cry and fall on the floor and walk out of church service into the same mess you came from. I'm hungry for people to see the promises of God at work in their lives, and not to just hear sermons from a bunch of ministers who want you to give them a high rating on the message. It's only when people can come to church, understand what's being preached, go, do and see manifestation can we say that the Word works. I'm talking about tasting, touching and seeing manifestation.

Now if you want a show, don't come to my church because you'll be in the wrong place. The Body of Christ has canceled amateur night at the theater. People don't want a show anymore, they want some Word that will go from the Bible into their hearts, and be reflected in their lives so they can say that manifestation time has indeed come!

I've been called to teach the Word of God with simplicity and understanding, and I won't quit until people understand it completely. I'm believing God for a fleet of airplanes so I can take the ministry from our church, and send people all over the world to preach the gospel of understanding, in order for lives to be changed. I'm telling you it's manifestation time. It's time to get your healing, it's time to get out of debt, it's time for you to marry the person you've prayed to God about.

I know you've read about tithing from a different perspective in this book than you may have heard about before. I pray this information has changed your life, and made a mark that cannot be erased.

The Covenant Connector

BECOME A PARTNER WITH WORLD CHANGERS MINISTRIES!

There is power, fellowship and commitment in partnership. We invite you to become a partner with World Changers Ministries in fulfilling the vision the Lord has given Creflo A. Dollar Jr. to teach the Word of God with simplicity and understanding.

To become a partner, simply fill out the appropriate information on the order form below, and mail your postage paid response today!

Our partners are valued friends and supporters of this ministry. We don't take lightly our responsibility to you to pray, diligently seek the Word of God, and minister to you monthly in a personal letter. As an additional benefit of partnership, we will offer from time to time discounted products to you for your spiritual edification and growth.

We look forward to entering into a covenant relationship with you, and pray that the blessings of God will be manifested in your life.

REMEMBER, THERE IS POWER IN PARTNERSHIP!

I'd like to become a Vision Partner in prayer and financial support with World Changers Ministries, Inc.

Last Name	First Name	Middle initial

Street address		Apartment

City	State	Zip Code

You can count on me for a monthly pledge of $1,000 $500 $100 $50 $25

_____
enter dollar amount

I listen to the radio broadcast on:_____
                                    station call letters

I watch the television broadcast on:_____
                                    station call letters

ABOUT THE AUTHOR

Creflo A. Dollar Jr. was born and raised in College Park, Georgia. After graduating from Lakeshore High School, he obtained a Bachelor of Education degree with a concentration in History from West Georgia College in Carrollton, Georgia. He began his professional career as a high school teacher in the Fulton County school system. From there, he became an Educational Therapist for Brawner Psychiatric Institute of Atlanta.

In 1986, Creflo Dollar began to carry out the call which God had placed on his life, by starting World Changers Christian Center, a non-denominational church in College Park. He began the ministry at a local elementary school with only eight members. At that time, the ministry was small, and aimed at developing a solid foundation for the fulfillment of a larger vision. He now pastors a church of over 17,000 people, and is an internationally known author, teacher and conference speaker with a ministry that not only reaches the local community, but also spans the globe. He can be seen and heard throughout the world on the "Changing Your World" broadcasts, via television and radio, and while conducting worldwide crusades.

Creflo Dollar and his wife, Taffi, live in Atlanta. They have four children — Gregory, Jordan, Alexandria and Lauren Grace.

OTHER BOOKS AND TAPES BY CREFLO A. DOLLAR JR.

BOOKS
Attitudes
Capturing the Reality of Heaven and Hell
Confidence: The Missing Substance of Faith
The Anointing to Live
The Color of Love
The Divine Order of Faith
The Sins of the Mouth
Understanding God's Purpose For The Anointing

TAPE SERIES
1997 Faith Convention: The Source of True Power
And Jesus Healed Them All
Christ in You: The Hope of Glory
Communication: The Master Key to An Anointed Family
Destroying the Root of Debt
Developing A Hunger And Thirst For The Anointed
     One And His Anointing
Due Season: When Will I Get From The Bottom To The
     Top?
Evicting The Devil From Your Home
God's Healing Word
Going Through The Furnace
How To Trouble Your Trouble
Living A Life of Diligence
Obedience As A Life
Passing The Test With Joy, Peace and Praise
Seven Steps to Prayer That Bring Results
SOS! Help, My Flesh Needs Discipline

TAPE SERIES (Continued)

The Burden-Removing, Yoke-Destroying Power of God
The Divine Order of Biblical Prosperity: 14 Practical Steps
      To Prospering in God
The Divine Order of Faith
The Importance of Seeking God
The Keys to Unlock The Anointing
The Laws That Govern Life
The Power and Authority Over Demonic Forces
The Reality of Redemption
The Revelation of Christ, The Anointed One
What Is The Kingdom of God?

THE SINNER'S PRAYER

Father, in the name of Jesus, I confess right now, and realize that I am a sinner. I repent of all my sins. I make an 180-degree turn away from all my sins. I change my heart, I change my mind, I change my direction, and I turn toward Jesus Christ. I confess with my mouth that God raised Jesus from the dead, and I believe in my heart that Jesus is alive and operates in my life. I thank you Lord that I am saved. Amen.

STEPS TO SALVATION
1.   Admit, recognize that you are a sinner. Psalm 51:5
2.   Repentance. 1 John 1:9
3.   Confession. Romans 10:9-10
4.   Baptisms - Water/Holy Spirit. Matthew 3:6
5.   Obedience to the Word of God. 1 John 5:3

SEVEN STEPS TO RECEIVING THE BAPTISM OF THE HOLY SPIRIT
1.   Understand that the Holy Spirit was poured out on the day of Pentecost. Acts 2:38
2.   The born-again experience is the only qualification necessary for receiving the Holy Spirit baptism. Acts 2:38
3.   The laying on of hands is scriptural. Acts 8:17

4. Know what to expect. Acts 19:6

5. Disregard all fears about receiving a counterfeit for the Holy Spirit. Luke 11:11-13

6. Open your mouth as an act of faith to receive the Holy Spirit. Ephesians 5:18-19

7. Let all things be done decently, and in order. 1 Corinthians 14:33.